Editorial Project Manager
Mara Ellen Guckian

Editor in Chief
Brent L. Fox, M. Ed.

Creative Director
Sarah M. Fournier

Cover Artist
Diem Pascarella

Illustrator
Sarah Kim

Imaging
Amanda R. Harter

Publisher
Mary D. Smith, M.S. Ed.

Teacher Created Resources
12621 Western Avenue
Garden Grove, CA 92841
www.teachercreated.com
ISBN: 978-1-4206-2147-1

Made in U.S.A.

Table of Contents

This book belongs to:

Introduction

Watch Me Learn: Cursive Writing Practice will help young writers learn proper letter formation for each letter of the alphabet using a simple "trace and write" format. Each cursive alphabet letter has its own page. Uppercase and lowercase letters are first traced and then written freehand.

Getting Started

Set aside a special time each day to practice and, if possible, establish a quiet "work space" free of other distractions. Encourage writers to hold their pens or pencils and paper correctly and to sit up at a desk or table to help them form letters properly. Most importantly, work together to make this practice time special.

- Point out that the arrows show the starting place and the direction to go to write each letter.
- Only a few cursive letters require a second stroke. Use the numbers to determine which line is written first when more than one continuous line is required for a letter.
- Encourage new writers to try to make continuous lines when tracing and writing each letter.
- Use the solid and dashed lines to help guide proper formation. Notice where each letter starts and stops and where lines are crossed.

Follow up each day's letter practice by acknowledging the young writer's efforts. Focus on the different aspects of the letters or words written:

- Is more than one line required to form a letter?
- Is the letter you practiced in your name?
- Which letters are the most fun to write?

Once writers are comfortable writing the letters of the alphabet, they can trace and write two- and three-letter words. Larger words are introduced by focusing on vowel or consonant blends before writing the whole word.

As cursive skills and confidence improve, the practice words become longer. Common words such as number words, the days of the week, and months of the year are practiced. Next, it is time to move on to the sentence pages. Note that the lines for writing sentences are smaller to help young writers transition to traditional writing paper. The last pages of the book allow writers to show what they have learned as they write about themselves.

Let's get started!

Name: ____

Name: ______________________________

Name: ______________________________

A A A A A A A

A

A

a a a a a a a a

a

a

Name: ______________________________

Bb

B B B B B B B

B

B

b b b b b b b b

b

b

Name: ______________________________

Cc

corn

Name: ______________________________

Name: ______________________________

elephant

Name: ______________________________

Ff

frog

2 3 1

F F F F F F F

F

F

f f f f f f f f

f

f

Name: ______________________________

Gg

grapes

Name: ______________________________

hippopotamus

Name: ______________________________

Ii

ice cream

I I I I I I I

I

I

2

1 *i i i i i i i i*

i

i

Name: ______________________________

Jj

jet

Name: ____________________

Kk

K K K K K K K

K

K

k k k k k k k k

k

k

Name: ____________________

L L L L L L L

L

L

l l l l l l l l

l

l

Name: ______________________________

Name: ______________________________

Name: ______________________________

Name: ______________________________

Pp

peas in a pod

p p p p p p p

p

p

p p p p p p p p

p

p

Name: ______________________________

Qq

quail

Q Q Q Q Q Q Q

Q

Q

q q q q q q q q

q

q

Name: ______________________________

Rr

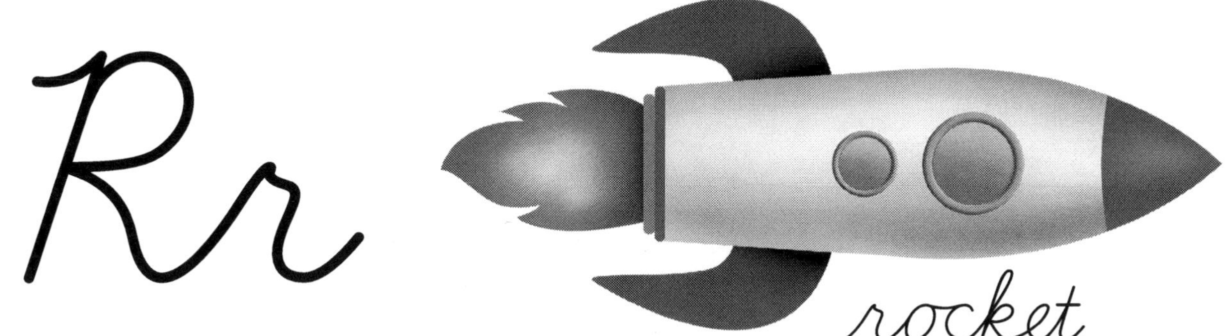

rocket

R R R R R R R

R

R

r r r r r r r r

r

r

Name: ____________________

Name: ____________________

Tt

tiger

2 1

T T T T T T T

T

T

2 1

t t t t t t t t

t

t

Name: ____________________

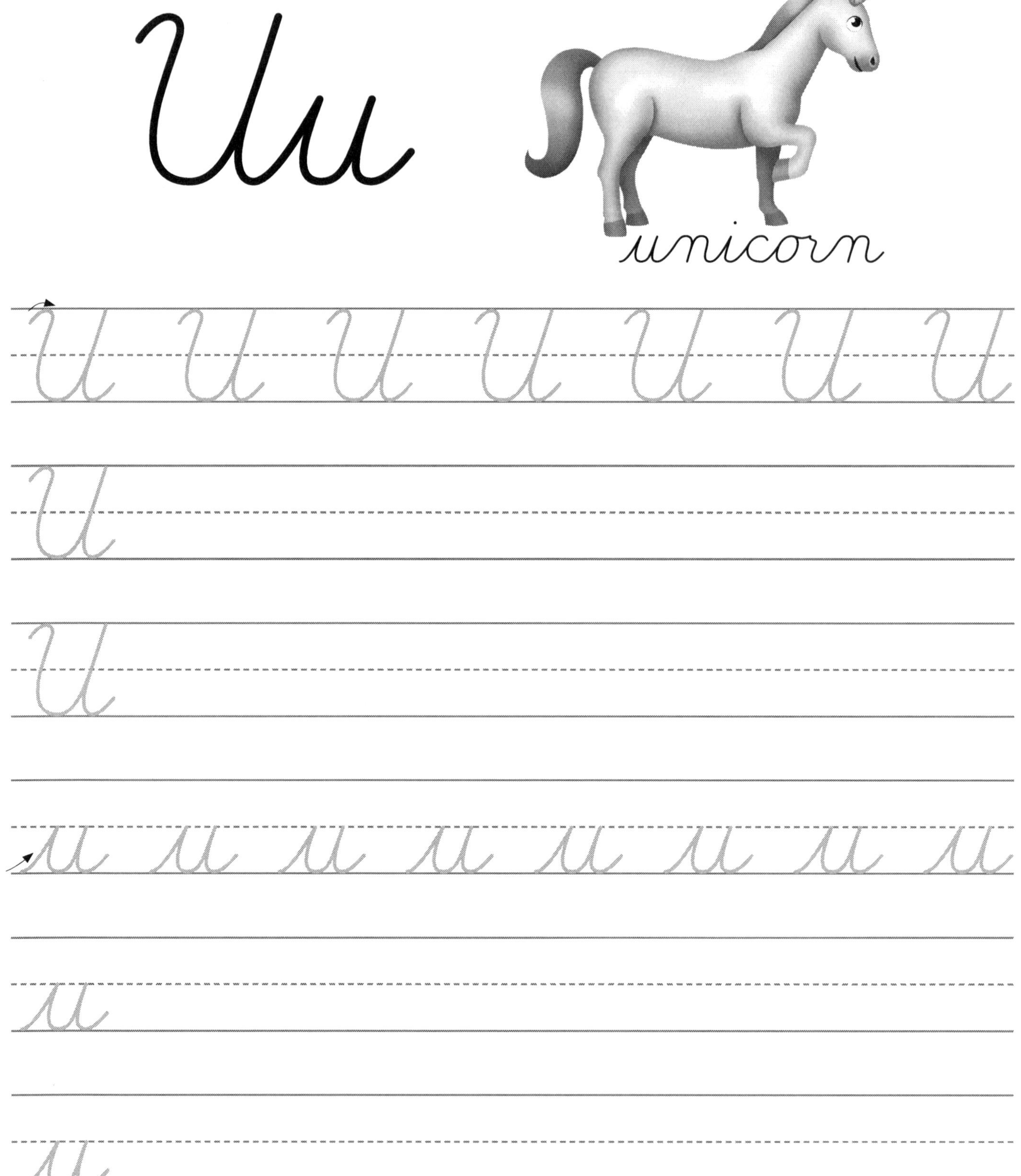

Name: ______________________________

Vv

violin

Name: ______________________________

Name: ______________________________

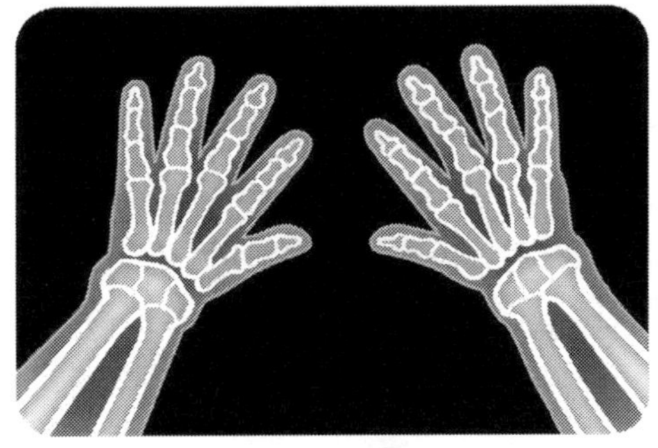

x-ray

Name: ______________________________

Yy

yo-yo

Name: ______________________________

Z z

zebra

Name: ______________________________

A B C D

E F G H

I J K L

M N O

P Q R

S T U

V W X

Y Z

Name: ____________________

a b c d

e f g h

i j k l

m n o

p q r

s t u

v w x

y z

Name: ____________________

am am

an an

as as

at at

be be

by by

do do

go go

Name: ____________________

he he

if if

in in

is is

it it

me me

my my

no no

Name: ______________________________

of of

on on

or or

so so

to to

up up

us us

we we

Name: ______________________________

ant

bat

car

dog

egg

fan

gum

hen

Name: ______________________________

ice

jar

key

leg

mop

nap

oar

pan

Name: ______________________________

ram

sun

tag

ump

van

web

yak

zoo

Name: ______________________________

bl bl bl bl

block

cl cl cl cl

clap

fl fl fl fl

flower

gl gl gl gl

gloves

Name: ______________________________

dr dr dr dr

dragon

gr gr gr gr

grapes

mp mp mp mp

lamp

tw tw tw tw

twig

Name: ______________________________

wh wh wh wh

whale

sh sh sh sh

sheep

sn sn sn sn

snake

fr fr fr fr

frog

Name: ______________________________

cc cc cc cc

soccer

rr rr rr rr

mirror

ss ss ss ss

possum

tt tt tt tt

mitten

Name: ______________________________

ai ai

hair hair

ai ai

pail pail

ay ay

hay hay

ea ea

seal seal

Name: ______________________________

ie ie

pie pie

oa oa

boat boat

oe oe

toe toe

oi oi

boil boil

Name: ______________________________

io io

lion lion

ue ue

blue blue

ou ou

ours ours

ui ui

fruit fruit

Name: ______________________________

ee ee

tree tree

ee ee

deer deer

oo oo

boot boot

uu uu

vacuum

Name: ______________________________

sch sch school

str str string

scr scr screw

spl spl splash

Name: ______________________________

thr thr three

spr spr sprout

nch nch inch

tch tch watch

Name: ______________________

Who

Why

Will

How

What

When

Where

Which

Name: ______________________

Because because

Since since

First first

Next next

Name: ______________________________

Create create

Share share

Help help

Listen listen

Name: ________________________________

0 zero zero zero

1 one one one

2 two two two

3 three three three

Name: ____________________

4 four four four

5 five five five

6 six six six

7 seven seven

Name:

8 eight eight eight

9 nine nine nine

10 ten ten ten

1 2 3 4 5 6 7 8 9 10

Name: ______________________________

Sunday

Monday

Tuesday

Wednesday

Name: ______________________________

Thursday

Friday

Saturday

weekend

Write your favorite day of the week on the line below.

Name: ______________________________

today today

tomorrow

yesterday

Name: ______________________________

January

February

March

April

Name: ____________________

May

June

July

August

Name: ______________________________

September

October

November

December

Name:

New Year's Day

Lunar New Year

MLK Jr. Day

Valentine's Day

Name: ____________________

President's Day

St. Patrick's Day

April Fool's Day

Easter

Name: ___________________________

Memorial Day

Fourth of July

Labor Day

Halloween

Name: ____________________

Veterans Day

Thanksgiving

Hanukkah

Christmas

Name: ______________________________

Today is your day!

Believe in yourself.

Do what you love.

Dream big!

Write your favorite saying on the line below.

Name: ______________________

Be brave.

Always be kind.

Try new things.

You have what it takes.

Write the sentence from above that is most important to you.

Name: ______________________________

Every day is a fresh

start.

Together we can change

the world.

Name: ______________________________

Smile at everyone you
see today.

Help clean up a mess
you didn't make.

Name: ____________________

A deer is on our deck!

It's eating our picnic.

What should we do?

Let's make some noise.

What would you do? Write your answer on the line below.

Name: ______________________________

I want to plant a

prickly pear.

It will need sun and

water to grow.

Name: ____________________

Do you see the goose
on the moose?

They are both loose
by the tree.

Name: ______________________________

I can't wait to go to

the beach!

Should we bring our

fins and masks?

Name: ______________________________

Dolphins and whales

are mammals.

An octopus has eight

limbs and a beak.

Name: ____________________

Would you rather...

swim, skate, or ski?

read, dance, or sing?

eat donuts or cookies?

play soccer or flag football?

Write your favorite of the activities listed above on this line.

Name: ______________________________

First Name

Last Name

Age—Write the number word.

Birthdate

Street Address

City

State and Zip Code

Phone Number

Name of School Grade

Name: ____________________

Things to Do

Place to Go

Holiday

Animals

Colors

Foods

Game to Play

Song

Sports

Name: ______________________________

Draw and write about your favorite time of year.

Name: ______________________________

Write about some things you hope to do as you grow older.

Name: ____________________

Made in the USA
Columbia, SC
29 April 2025